Se

for Mums

The little book to help you care for yourself while caring for your baby

By Dr Charlotte Hartley-Jones

DClinPsy

Copyright © 2016 by Charlotte Hartley-Jones. All rights reserved.

ISBN: 978-1-326-79542-9

This book or any portion thereof may not be reproduced or used in any manner whatsoever without the express written permission of the publisher except for the use of brief quotations in a book review.

Disclaimer: The information is this book is not intended as a substitute for professional medical, psychological or psychiatric treatment. Always seek the advice of a health care provider if you have any concerns about your mental or physical health.
www.selfkindnessformums.com
www.charlottehartleyjones.com
First edition

Acknowledgements

Thank you to all the mums and dads who have contributed to my understanding of self-kindness for mums, who test drove the exercises and read drafts. Thanks to Isobel Gammer whose research project I am helping supervise looking at self-compassion for mums as part of her clinical psychology doctorate; your thoughtfulness and comments helped me clarify some of the points in this book. Thank you to my husband who as a clinical psychologist, mindfulness teacher and caring husband and father, has been an invaluable sounding board and extremely useful editor and motivator. Finally, thanks to my three children who have all taught me many lessons about being a mother. May we continue to learn together about the joys and pains of being human and help each other remember the lessons of kindness above all else.

Table of Contents

Chapter One. Introduction 1

Chapter Two. What is Self-Kindness? 8

Chapter Three. Birth 14

Chapter Four. Feeding, Sleeping and the First Few Days 20

Chapter Five. Emotional Roller Coaster 29

Chapter Six. Other People's Opinions 36

Chapter Seven. Shaking Hands with the Inner Critic 43

Chapter Eight. New Mum Identity 51

Chapter Nine. Relationships 58

Chapter Ten. Expectations versus reality 66

Chapter Eleven. Going Forward 72

Chapter Twelve. Additional Resources 76

Chapter One

Introduction

Babies are not born with manuals. That big blob of placenta that follows them out does not hold any Holy Grail list of personalised 'how to's' (that would be handy right?). Yet we mothers can sometimes feel there *is* a way we should be mothering and due to our own inadequacies we just keep missing the target.

It's as if we believe on a subconscious level that the manual *does* exist, we just haven't worked out how to read it yet. We can sometimes end up having thoughts such as:

'If only we could be more like X (friend, sister, woman at the bus stop) maybe our baby would sleep more.'

'If only we could work out how to feed our baby

properly then maybe our baby wouldn't be so windy.'

'If only we could wind our baby better then perhaps he or she wouldn't have just vomited all over our last clean top.'

'If only we were organised enough to carry two (or maybe three) nappy bags with us then we wouldn't have run out of nappies in the middle of poomageddon.'

'If only we were cool and casual enough to never have to carry a huge nappy bag, buggy, sling and five changes of clothes then we wouldn't feel like a pack horse.'

'If only we were more disciplined then we wouldn't need to eat cake every day and spoonfuls of chocolate spread out the jar.'

Maybe you have different examples (and perhaps aren't susceptible to the cake and chocolate spread) but it is likely that if you are a mum you may recognise the general idea.

In reality is likely that since your baby arrived you've had to adapt to a new lifestyle, learn new skills, function on very little sleep and probably face conflicting advice from others, all while recovering from the birth and dealing with emotional highs and lows. In addition to all this, your relationships may have suffered, and friendships might have changed.

Despite managing so much at a time when your resources are low from lack of sleep and hormonal changes, have you noticed a tendency to be self-critical or judge yourself harshly? Perhaps you feel guilty about things you haven't done for your baby, or things you have done, or the way you have felt, or haven't felt, or things you have thought, or haven't thought. If you recognise yourself in any of this, you are certainly not alone.

The idea behind this little book is to help lessen the grip of some of the 'shoulds', and 'musts' that tend to raise their heads when a baby is born. These 'shoulds and 'musts' can lead us to feel worse about ourselves and others. Examples of them could be:

- 'I *should* always get feeding right otherwise I'm a failure.'
- 'I *must* get the baby to sleep without feeding her otherwise I'm setting up bad habits.'
- 'My partner *must* understand how exhausted I am and what I need otherwise our relationship is doomed.'

Letting go of these 'shoulds' and 'musts' can allow us to appreciate the small window of time we have when our babies are young without feeling so overburdened by guilt and self-criticism.

Understanding the importance of being kind to ourselves can sometimes be hard to grasp. *What if I am too soft on myself? How will I ever motivate myself? What if I just want to sit on the sofa and eat chocolates all day*? If you have such thoughts, it's understandable, especially in societies that applaud success, striving and 'holding it together' over more gentle acceptance of who we are. Sometimes we can associate being kind to ourselves with failing or giving up and that can be uncomfortable. However, being able to be kind to ourselves may help us:

- soothe the 'inner critic', self-doubt, confusion, and disorientation that can accompany the arrival of a baby;
- find peace with our own parenting style;
- deal with conflicting advice;
- avoid comparing ourselves negatively to others;
- look after ourselves in the midst of chronic tiredness;
- bring gentle understanding to the range of thoughts and feelings that often accompany motherhood;
- find ways to pause and soak up the special moments;
- have better relationships with our partners, friends, family members and children;

- accept the impact motherhood can have on us.

Increasing our care for ourselves can also lead to us being more patient with others. And as an extra bonus if our children see us being kind to ourselves it is likely they will start practicing self-kindness towards themselves too.

However, even if we do think self-kindness is a good idea intellectually, understanding alone often isn't always enough which is why this book has been designed to help you *practice* being kinder to yourself. The information and exercises have been developed drawing on various psychological frameworks, research and theories, e.g. cognitive behavioural therapy (CBT), mindfulness, narrative therapy and compassionate therapy approaches. The chapters and exercises are short, designed to help you access and carry them out them out easily, fitting into life with a baby.

The book is not intended as a method of banishing self-judgment, guilt or difficult feelings, as these are human reactions to life's challenges. Instead it aims to help new mums and old hand mums with noticing that they are not alone with difficult thoughts and feelings and with boosting self-kindness and dampening down self-criticism.

The quotes and exercises in this book are anonymised adaptations and amalgamations from my work with mothers (running self-kindness sessions, carrying out research and providing therapy), my experience and knowledge as a clinical psychologist and mindfulness researcher, and my own struggles and learning as a mum.

No single book could sum up the complexities of motherhood for all women and there are many unrepresented views here, but my hope is that some of the ideas, quotes or exercises can help you find a place in your hearts for yourself while you are busy with the important job of being a mother. You might not want to try all the exercises, and that's fine, they are suggestions offered in the spirit of exploration and invitation- the last thing mums need are any more rules or 'shoulds'!

Chapter Two

What is Self-Kindness?

Being human provides plenty of opportunities for difficult experiences and painful feelings which can benefit from gentleness and soothing. Self-kindness provides a way to give yourself the sort of soothing and friendly care you would offer a loved one. It is not the same as over indulgence or pity and does not mean always giving yourself an 'easy ride' or ignoring mistakes. Instead, it is being able to accept your humanness and being gentle instead of harsh. It is about being a friend to yourself rather than a harsh critic, knowing when you need a little motivating and when you need to give yourself a break.

When you become a mum there are many moments when self-kindness could help. There are moments in the middle of the night where some of us may have stood at a dark window feeling we are all alone, moments we may have wondered whether to leave the house and keep walking, moments when we may have felt consumed by anger, sadness or guilt. There are moments when we may have thought everyone else is doing a better job than us. If you have had moments like these, they show that you are human, they show that you are learning new skills and most likely doing it all on a crazily little amount of sleep.

What does being kind to yourself mean to you? Does it seem like a good idea? It can make sense to some people but be a painful thought for others. It can seem a great idea in theory but you might wonder what you can do to put it into practice. Or sometimes you might switch between thinking it's a good idea, thinking it's a waste of your attention and worrying that it might be actively unhelpful. Whatever your reaction is, especially if you have any doubts about the value of being kinder to yourself you could give this book and the exercises a try and see from your own experience what difference they make.

Below are examples of comments from mothers

about what self-kindness means to them. Some of the quotes may resonate with you and some will not, but the idea of including quotes is to provide access to the thoughts and feelings of other mums. By getting to see what other mums have felt about the topics in this book you can hopefully feel less alone with some of the 'big' emotions and issues of motherhood. Sometimes it can be helpful to know that we are not alone in our experiences. Although we are all unique individuals, many of our thoughts, feelings and reactions are likely to be shared or similar to others. The quotes are offered without commentary so they can be flicked through and mulled over by you in peace. Some you may skim over and never think of again, others may require more consideration and perhaps strike a chord.

***

I didn't have a chance to consider being kind to myself when my first baby was born. It was all consuming- physically, emotionally and practically.

I tried a loving kindness meditation once. It was really intense and I cried. It showed me how hard I am on myself.

Since having a baby I've questioned myself over every little choice, it's like I've lost the ability to trust myself and I'm not always kind to myself about that, I'm annoyed at myself.

Sometime I don't think I deserve any kindness.

Self-kindness makes me think of hot baths and dressing gowns. Curling up on the sofa with a blanket. I miss doing that.

Self-kindness sounds a bit 'floaty' or 'hippyish', it doesn't really fit with me.

The idea of self-kindness makes me feel a bit lonely as if no-one else is going to be kind to me.

To me it's about giving yourself a break. Life is

too short to beat yourself up all the time.

***

Exercise 1

Imagine someone you know came to you and said that they were exhausted, hadn't slept or eaten properly for weeks (or months or even years). Imagine they told you that over the last few months or weeks they had been bruised and aching, confused and tearful. You would probably want to reach out and help them. You might want to give them a big hug, listen to them, speak gently to them, perhaps send them off to bed for a nap, and cook them a nice meal. However, if you are a new mother, have you been able to turn even a proportion of this kindly care and attention to yourself whilst in the midst of nurturing your baby? For this exercise see if you can stop and notice the next time you give yourself a harsh time and ask; would you speak to a friend like that? Try speaking to yourself how you would to someone else (this might be out loud or just to yourself). At first it might be hard to think of what you might 'say' to yourself so some ideas could be:

'You're doing great as you are',

'It's no wonder you are having a hard time right now, you are exhausted'

'Hang in there, you're doing great'

'It's ok, you're ok'

At first it may feel a little forced and unnatural but it might just help you send a bit of care your own way while you are busy sending so much care to your little person.

Chapter Three

Birth

If you have recently given birth, the best case scenario physically is that you've probably got some bruising, bleeding, sore breasts and tiredness to contend with. The best case emotionally might be that the process was profound and full of joy. However, moving on from the best case scenario opens up a huge range of experiences and feelings you may be struggling with such as a sore C-section scar, incontinence, tears, cuts, traumatic memories, disappointment, exhaustion, or shame.

Absolutely every birth is unique and no matter how many times we might have heard friends speak of their babies' births, it's very hard to prepare for your own baby's birth. The impact of giving birth can resonate like ripples under the surface of those first few months and even years. It can be good to take a moment to give yourself a big pat on the back for getting your baby out into the world or for bringing a baby into your family, however it happened and however long ago it happened.

There can often be disappointment around a birth that didn't go as hoped for, but you did it. You made a baby, grew a baby and got that baby out. That in itself is worthy of some imaginary flag waving and party tooting, yet you probably barely had time to take a breath before you are onto the nappy changing, sleeplessness and round the clock feeding.

Here are some examples of comments other mothers have made when they looked back at their babies births:

***

I remember crying and saying 'I can't do it'. I was desperate for someone to take over for me but knew they couldn't.

Because we adopted our son, I didn't get the chance to give birth to him and I feel envious of other mums discussing their births. Our 'birth story' started with the decision to adopt. It includes all the paperwork, assessments, and emotional ups and downs.

We bought one of the co-sleeper cots that attaches to the side of the bed but my episiotomy was so sore I couldn't sit down or walk properly let alone scoot up and down the bed. It hadn't occurred to me that I wouldn't be able to walk after having a 'natural birth'.

We only stayed in hospital one night but it felt like weeks. All day there were people pulling back the curtain all offering advice on how I should be breast feeding. There were doctors, midwives, students, peer support workers, a seemingly endless procession of people expecting me to bare my nipples at them so they could all scrutinise and comment.

I had her at home in the waterpool, the midwife cleared up and made us tea and toast to have in bed. It was perfect. Sometimes I feel guilty when so many of my friends had such a tough time.

When they told me my husband had to go home I cried. I couldn't believe I was going to be left alone in that place with the baby to manage on my own.

I kept having flashbacks of the birth, little things would remind me all the time and I'd be back there re-living it.

There was so much blood afterwards. I felt like it was a full time job dealing with the pads and yet no-one had ever told me about that.

I felt cheated. Where was my lovely, peaceful birth? I didn't even feel happy when I eventually got to hold my baby. I started off motherhood feeling like a failure but didn't tell anyone.

***

Exercise 2

The idea for this exercise is to get yourself an object to remind you of your intention to be kind to yourself, to remind yourself that you are doing it, you are being a mum however hard the birth was, however many tears you might have cried over the baby's head, however snappy you have been or however exhausted you are. You might choose something you already own e.g. a special piece of jewellery, an ornament, a stone, or you may decide to make a deliberate trip to the shops to choose something. You could get a crystal, a furry toy or a plastic animal. It doesn't matter what the object is as long as you feel it could represent your plan to be kind to yourself. Put your chosen object wherever you will notice it the most either throughout the day or at the times you most need to be reminded. You might choose to put it by your bed, by where the baby sleeps (which may or may not be the same place), by where you most frequently feed your baby, or by the bathroom sink so that when you visit the toilet, brush your teeth or have a shower you will notice it. You could keep it in your pocket or in your handbag or nappy bag, or it might even be a brooch that you could pin to your clothes.

Whatever you choose, wherever you put it, and even if you don't choose to do this exercise, take a moment now to remind yourself of how far you have already come…whether your baby is one day old, one year old or even 30 years old!

Chapter Four

Feeding, Sleeping and the First Few Days

Feeding and sleeping can feel big issues from day one until...well, years later. But there is nothing like those first days (or weeks or months) with your new baby to have the potential to leave you punching pillows in frustration, crying at random things and snapping at your partner. It can be so hard learning how to feed a baby and working out how you and your family are going to adjust to life with a new-born, and yet many mums can end up feeling like a failure if it's not going 'right'.

Why would you just 'know' how to look after this baby and easily work out how to use the car seat, buggy, steriliser, sling? How can you have just magically woken up the day after your baby's birth knowing everything about keeping a tiny human alive? It's all so new and a massive learning curve.

If you breastfeed you might be thinking there 'must' be a neater, simpler way than this messy, confusing process you and your baby are on. Or, if you are bottle feeding, you might wonder whether there is a 'better' way to organise the cleaning, co-ordinating, and packing of bottles to go out, or to do the night feeds.

However, despite our fantasies of what other mums are experiencing, the struggle *is* often the reality for many mums, and comparing ourselves to the glimpses we get of other mums and babies is often not helpful. You and your baby (or babies) are a unique partnership both learning so much right now.

Neither of you got any memo on the intricate details of how to do any of this stuff. If you can be gentle with yourself in these early days, at least you can soften some of the impact of any inner judgements you may have about doing things 'better'. It can sometimes help to remember to just focus on each moment at a time; to get through each feed or each minute of the night rather than looking ahead too much. If you do find it helpful to try and focus on the moment you could have a phrase you repeat to yourself like 'just one moment at a time'. If you don't find that idea helpful maybe just reminding yourself 'we'll get through this' or 'we're doing ok' could be phrases worth trying.

In the big scheme of life everything changes fast when our babies are small but in the everyday minutiae of post-birth, a few minutes can sometimes feel like a mountain. The following mum quotes sum up some of the mountains and solutions new mums found in the craziness of the early days.

***

When I was pregnant I'd looked forward to being able to lie on my tummy to sleep again. What I hadn't reckoned with was the mounds of pain my breasts had morphed into. At times I couldn't even sleep on my side because of pain with engorgement. Sometimes I had to sleep almost sitting up.

I was given a breastfeeding cover but never used it. I thought that I shouldn't use one, I felt as if using one was being wimpy, and not supporting a sisterhood of breast-feeders. Looking back I wish I'd just used the cover. I didn't like flashing my boobs in public.

My husband made me lunch when he made his own lunch for work. It was so helpful and I felt like I was being looked after when he wasn't there.

I couldn't 'nap when the baby naps'. I tried it a couple of times and the pain of getting into bed for a lovely nap and being woken up just as I was falling to sleep was too horrible.

I had to sleep whenever I could, I took every chance. I made myself ignore the pull to have a shower or brush my teeth and I just went to bed.

Our sleeping arrangements were totally haphazard. I would have a few minutes on the sofa sometimes (day or night), my husband slept on an air bed or the sofa or maybe the bed. The baby slept wherever we could get her to sleep and we just did shifts.

We put a sign on the door that said 'baby sleeping, please don't knock, any parcels can be left under recycle box'.

I know this sounds ungrateful but I hated being given flowers. I couldn't get myself dressed or brush my teeth, let alone find a clean vase, cut the ends of some flowers, arrange them and then manage to deal with them once they were dead. Friends and family had wanted to express their love and joy by sending beautiful bouquets of flowers but all we had done with them was leave them by the front door.

I think my friends and family didn't want to crowd us after the baby was born so we didn't have many visitors but looking back I realise I felt quite isolated and would have liked to see everyone.

***

Exercise 3

Once you have a baby it can be hard to do the things that used to help you feel good. Maybe you used to like having a long hot bath, going for a walk, a bike ride, gardening, having a big night out at the pub, mastering a new recipe, reading a book, going to bed early (or really late and having a massive lie in), browsing round the shops, or even going to work. Although some of these things might be impossible with a baby, with a little adaption you may be able to find a window to do something for you (even if you have a baby accompaniment). Doing things that help you feel good is not self-indulgent; if you have moments when you are feeling more relaxed, confident, happy or satisfied then this is likely to have positive knock on effects both for your well-being and your family.

For this exercise the task is to choose at least

one thing that you can do to consciously nurture yourself this week. You could choose something from the list below or come up with your own. Sometimes as parents we have to put in more effort and planning to nurture ourselves than we ever had to do before.

The list includes activities that you probably do anyway when you can (like perhaps having a shower or bath!) but the idea is to do it with the conscious recognition that it's just for *you*, that it's part of your intention to be kind to yourself while you are taking on so much.

- Go for a walk (it could be a few steps, a stroll round the block, or a country hike).
- Look out of a window and notice the trees, people, clouds, or whatever is there.
- Take five big deep breaths.
- Have a bath or shower.
- Use a facemask, paint your nails, put on moisturiser.
- Phone, text, email, or meet up with a friend.

- Listen to music.
- Paint a picture, do some colouring, draw something.
- Watch a film (if your baby is young enough you could watch it with them perhaps).
- Have your favourite supper or take away.
- Do some gardening (or perhaps visit a garden centre if you haven't got a garden or any plants).
- Connect with an old hobby.
- Try out a new recipe (or look up a new recipe if it's too much to cook something new right now).
- Drink a cup of tea, coffee, water slowly, really paying attention to it (even if you don't get to finish it; the half drank cup of tea is a common sign of being a parent!).
- Buy yourself a treat just for you (although if you would prefer to buy something for your baby that would be fine too).

Whatever you choose remember that it's your

moment to take a little care just for you. The more you try out this exercise the more it can strengthen your intention to take care of yourself while you are so busy taking care of a small someone else.

Chapter Five

Emotional Roller Coaster

Being a mother can be the best and worst of times. There can be profound moments of almost physical joy, love, connection and happiness, but also painful feelings of anger, frustration, boredom, loneliness, sadness, guilt, shock, jealousy and anxiety. How can you be kind and gentle with yourself in the midst of these whirling and competing emotions?

One of the first steps can be to recognise the difficult emotions, remind yourself that these are normal experiences for new mums and practice 'letting them be'. This means being able to label our emotions (which is sometimes harder than it seems) and not get too caught up in them, for example by practicing not allowing them to take over our actions. They are part of being human and especially part of being a mother.

For example, many mothers report feelings of anger, frustration and annoyance arising suddenly and forcefully, often in relation to crying babies. A helpful thing to remember about both thoughts and feelings is that they are *not* the same as actions.

Shouting or throwing something across the room are actions but thoughts and feelings are 'only' thoughts and feelings. To have a fleeting thought of walking out on your family or dropping your baby down the stairs is *not* the same as doing it and research has shown that experiencing shocking or strange thoughts throughout the course of a day is not unusual. However, these thoughts can cause problems if we start to believe that having such thoughts makes us a bad person or when we get fixated on the thoughts and emotions they bring up.

Being able to be kind to ourselves after anger, fear or sadness has visited allows us to avoid attributing them to being a 'bad' mother. You are not a bad mother because you have difficult or painful feelings. Difficult and painful feelings show us that we are human and often that we are being stretched; and motherhood certainly can stretch us in many directions at once!

If you are finding that you are acting out of your anger or even sadness in ways that are unhelpful, there are avenues that can help. Contacting your GP, family doctor or health visitor can be good ways of accessing more support.

Catching the positive moments (or the mini-peaks) of motherhood can also provide a buffer at more difficult times. They can help build a bank of positive memories to lean on when we are having a tough evening, day or week. A tip to help build your bank of positive mini-peaks is to stop right now and think back over today to try and remember a positive experience, feeling or thought that you've had. It might be you need to think back further than today and it might be the thought or feeling was very fleeting, but that's ok. Sometimes we need to start really small like a moment when our teeth felt clean or we didn't feel so sad or angry. The bigger peaks might be a moment when your baby smiled at you, you felt connected to your child, you felt the fresh air on your face or felt joy at the thought of someone coming to help you with the baby.

Here are some example comments from other mothers that might resonate with some of your experiences.

***

I was scared I wouldn't be able to keep the baby alive. What if she suffocated when she was asleep or she choked on something and I didn't notice? What if I dropped her?

I cried at anything. TV advertisements would set me off and as for news or charity pleas, I would be sobbing.

One night the baby was crying, I'd already fed him to sleep five times that night and I couldn't take it anymore. I lay on the floor and cried too. My partner heard us both and came to our rescue. We talked about how I was feeling and made an agreement that if I got near to feeling like that again I wake him up straight away.

Occasionally when the baby was tiny I would suddenly be hit by a wall of sadness. I would be fine and then suddenly, bang, there it was. After a while I realised it would mostly appear after a big breastfeeding session. In the end I put it down to hormones and that helped me feel better.

I was surprised how much having a baby made me fear my own death. I had imagined being worried for my baby's safety but I hadn't considered how I would be worried for my own life. The idea that I might die and my baby would grow without a mother would have me in tears especially at 3am in a dark house while breastfeeding.

I felt guilty about everything. And then I felt guilty about feeling guilty in case my baby picked up on it.

Everyone was pressurising me to take a break from looking after my baby. I know they were only doing it for my own good but I didn't want to. And then I felt bad for not wanting a break, as if I wasn't capable of helping myself when other people were all telling me what was best for me. I didn't feel ready and didn't feel that I was being listened to. I felt as if I was being 'soppy' feeling so anxious about being away from him. That phase didn't last forever and eventually I was ready to have some time to myself but the main thing that stands out to me now was how hard it was to try and explain it to everyone.

I felt so much disorientation, at times I felt like I was out of my body observing.

Before I go to sleep each night I try to think of three things that went well that day no matter how small they might be. It's helped me notice little positives that before I probably would have dismissed or not even registered.

I didn't make it to the toilet in time when my baby was a couple of weeks old. I was so ashamed I didn't want to tell anyone, and then I found out faecal incontinence is quite common and I was so relieved, I wished I had known about it earlier and saved myself from feeling so awful.

I'd like to bottle up a few hours of my baby now which I could re visit when I am older and he is a teenager or has left home. I know I will long for these snuggles, these smiles, this soft skin to stroke. But now I have him wanting me every hour of every day it's hard to always remember to appreciate it.

We had three rounds of IVF before we had Mathew and I feel as if I must always be grateful, must always be happy because of how much we longed for a baby. But I don't always feel grateful or happy.

***

Exercise 4
Get outside and breathe it in! Go outside and take a big breath of air in through you nose and out whichever way you like just notice the air coming into your nostrils and filling your body. That's it. That's the whole exercise.

Chapter Six

Other People's Opinions

New parents are surrounded by ideas and suggestions from friends, family, books, health professionals, magazines, television programmes and even strangers about how to bring up a baby. There are constant decisions to make and small choices to agonise over, so turning to outside sources for help is understandable. However, while we know babies don't come with a handbook, parenting books *are* continually published which offer 'instructions' on sleeping, feeding, and everything else baby related. These can be helpful when used to pick out the bits that fit with you and your baby, but can also add fuel to confusion and doubt, especially as different sources can offer differing and sometimes contradictory, advice.

You can end up feeling inadequate if you attempt to follow an idea and it doesn't work, or if you don't want to follow an idea, or if your baby doesn't do what the book says the baby will do. Being kind to yourself in the face of all the conflicting information can help you navigate all the advice that's available and hopefully find more peace with your own parenting decisions.

It can be difficult when friends and family have different ideas about how to look after a baby and it is rare to be given advice without an undercurrent of some sort of emotion or bigger issue. When this advice comes from people whose opinion we generally trust or who we love, it can be even harder to respond.

How can we tell our mother we don't agree with what she is suggesting when it might sound like we are criticising her parenting? How can we let our friends know that their well-meant 'tips' for getting a baby to sleep are showing up fundamental differences in child rearing approaches and don't suit us? How can we respond to strangers in the park who voice their opinions on why our toddler is lying face down on the roundabout screaming? How can we read a parenting book and not feel like a failure if we don't feel up to following the suggestions?

Noticing what opinions we react against, as well as which opinions we gravitate towards can help us develop and have trust in our own parenting path. We will all take different steps along this path and unsolicited opinions that we have strong reactions to are a gift as they can actually show us what we *don't* want and how we *don't* want to be. Here are some example quotes from other mums that show how they have experienced a range of different opinions.

***

A couple of friends said to me 'it gets better at three months'. When it didn't get better and the baby was waking every hour at 8 months I felt like a failure. I also felt cheated that they didn't know what they were talking about. Of course they did know what they were talking about in their experience, with their baby, but my baby was different.

When my baby wasn't latching and I couldn't get

her to take a bottle I spoke to a friend who told me she'd tried loads of bottles and only one type had worked. I ordered one of the bottles straight away and couldn't wait for it to arrive. I was so relieved we would have an end to the worry about whether she was getting enough milk. The bottle arrived two days later, I cracked it open, got it all ready and gave it to her. She screamed and writhed around in total refusal. I was so upset.

I spent the first few months of my baby's life Googling through the early hours. Some of the things I searched for were 'green poo', 'baby refusing feeds', 'baby awake for hours in the night', 'is it ok to use a dummy?', 'how to bottle feed', 'when to express' and many, many more. I read site after site after site and I enjoyed it. I never felt I could have too much information.

I was lent a couple of parenting books before my baby was born and read a little bit but decided it was stressing me out and I haven't read any since. I guess they are helpful for some people but we just muddled through.

We did some sleep training and it worked out well for us but I found it hard to talk to anyone about it without having to justify it.

I never told people how my baby was actually sleeping. Everyone seemed to have an option on how to make her sleep 'better' and actually I was happy the way it was, yes I was exhausted but I knew it wouldn't last forever, I wanted to be there for her whenever she needed me.

Some of my friends don't understand why I can't just get a babysitter and go out with them still. I think they feel a bit let down because that's what other mums they know do.

I felt judged by friends and family because I was breastfeeding all the time. People would make comments like 'surely he can't still be hungry' and 'why don't you give him a bottle so you can have a break', 'maybe he just wants to play, be cuddled, go to sleep' and 'he's old enough to have a bottle now'.

My mother-in-law thought the baby should be asleep at 7pm, should be fed on a schedule, and should never be rocked or fed to sleep. I had friends who thought babies should sleep next to the mum, should always be carried in slings (not buggies) and breastfeeding on demand was the only way to do it. I felt guilty about the different things I did depending on who I was with.

***

Exercise 5
If you keep a baby record book, write something about yourself in it. When your baby is older they will appreciate knowing more about their mum and you will get to remind yourself that you matter too and that you are an individual as much as your baby is. If the baby book is one with specific sections, you could write on the back of a page, on in the margins or add a section. You don't have to write anything profound or in great detail (although you could if you wanted to). You could just write

what your favourite meal at the moment is, what you used to do before you had your baby, or where your favourite travel destination is. Or you could add some old pictures of yourself in there with some captions. If you don't keep a baby record book, you could write on a piece of paper, in a card or on a blackboard. You could stick it on the fridge or on a wall to remind yourself that every day you are on your own journey and are having your own 'mum milestones', just as your baby is having his or hers.

Chapter Seven

Shaking Hands with the Inner Critic

The inner critics that lurk inside many of us can really go to town when we become mums. They thrive on sleepless nights, low energy and emotional confusion. They can be heard clearest when we compare ourselves negatively to others and when we feel we aren't living up to an (often impossible) ideal we've set ourselves.

Some people have raging inner critics that can be vicious and attacking, and some don't have any tendency to judge themselves harshly at all. Most of us are probably somewhere between those two extremes for all sorts of reasons (e.g. genetics, temperament, upbringing, life experiences).

Fear, doubt or worry often accompany judgments and self-criticism. For new mums this fear can be about not doing the very best for our baby. We might berate ourselves for not having the birth we planned, not being able to breastfeed, or for choosing to formula feed. We might feel bad that we are sometimes angry with the baby, that we don't want to face bathing our wriggly, slippery bundles, that we haven't made it out the house in days, or that getting dressed seems a momentous task.

We might agonise over sleep issues: to do a routine or 'demand' feed; to rock the baby to sleep or actively avoid it? We may have partners, friends, or family members telling us that we could set up 'bad habits', or read about how 'breast is best' while feeding our babies from a carton and feel guilt and a sense of shame that can manifest in self-criticism.

Some people worry that if they let go of their inner critic they might get lazy or let their standards slip. Perhaps you feel if you don't keep a close eye on your mistakes that you will miss an opportunity to do your best. Being self-aware doesn't have to cause difficulties, but when it leads to self-criticism, painful feelings or negative behaviours it can cause problems. For new mums, repeated harsh self-criticism can lead to low mood, anxiety, not enjoying time with your baby, and even depression.

Self-critical thoughts can maintain negative cycles whereby our judgemental thoughts can lead to negative feelings which can lead to more self-critical thoughts. These thoughts and feelings can affect our behaviour and end up perpetuating a vicious circle.

Modern scientific techniques have recently shown that the act of sending ourselves kind thoughts actually impact brain patterns. The way we talk to ourselves has the power to influence the way our brains work. Our brains respond to both our own criticisms and our own soothing, in a similar way to if someone else was criticising or soothing us.

So if instead of criticism we can relate to ourselves with more understanding, encouragement and gentleness, we can loosen the inner critic and let kindness be our guide. One way to approach this can be to think what the wisest, kindest person you could ever imagine would say in response to your worries or self-criticism. For example:

You: *'I'm so useless, I haven't done the dishes from yesterday, the house is a mess, I'm a mess, the baby is crying.*

Imagined wisest, kindest person: *'You are not useless, you are tired, and you are busy caring for your baby, what a lovely mummy you are. No wonder you haven't been able to do the dishes and no wonder the house is a mess, you are keeping a new human being alive. Never mind about the dishes for now, they will get done, what do you need right now? What will help you get through this moment?'*

You could try imagining what this wisest kindest person might say to you the next time you feel inadequate or stressed. It can also help to remember other mums may be struggling with similar feelings especially behind closed doors. Here are some example comments which demonstrate some of the ways we mums can give ourselves a hard time.

***

I stopped breastfeeding at four months. I wasn't up to feeding round the clock. Some of the mothers I knew breastfed their babies constantly but I couldn't. I questioned what it was about me that meant I had 'given up', why was I not strong enough and they were? I took it as a personal failure.

I felt fat. Other mums seemed to be wearing 'normal clothes' and I was still in my maternity clothes. I used to tell myself I was fat and disgusting, even though when I look back I realise I was very harsh on myself, I'd just had a baby, no wonder I wasn't looking my best.

My baby screamed every time she was in the car seat. None of the other mums I knew had that problem. I felt like there was something I wasn't doing right. Why couldn't she just sleep in the car like the other babies?

I was the first in my group of friends to have children and over the weeks and months I started to realise I couldn't keep up. I missed birthdays, forgot to text back, didn't remember important things about their lives and I was so cross with myself.

I hated having my photo taken because I thought I looked washed out, tired and old. I was critical about my appearance all the time.

Someone I knew used to go out with only a tiny bag and her baby in the sling. She always looked so casual about having a baby. I used to feel inadequate because I would be there with a buggy, load of stuff and a bulging bag, and I still felt unprepared. Looking back I realise it really didn't matter, but at the time it tapped into some old insecurities from school days about not being 'cool'.

My antenatal group have a morning text round up of how the night has been. I have started to think there is something wrong with me and my baby as we seem to be waking so much more than any of them.

Everyone else seemed to be managing better than me. They had better nappy bags, and nicer buggies. They had better partners, better in-laws, better houses. They had better tactics to get their babies to sleep. Basically I just thought I was a rubbish mum and couldn't do anything right.

I took my baby to swimming classes when he was tiny and found the logistics of getting us both undressed, into the pool, then getting us both dry and dressed impossible. I used to look around the changing room at these other mothers getting on with it and coping, and I would feel really bad that I couldn't manage. In reality I was managing, but at the time I didn't see it like that.

***

Exercise 6

This exercise is for wherever you see bubbles, for example you may see them in the washing up bowl, the bath or in a muddy puddle. You might see them when a child blows bubbles, when you wash your hands or where waves crash in the sea. Perhaps there will be bubbles in your next drink; your coffee, milkshake, fizzy water or even champagne? The idea is to just notice whenever you see some bubbles from now on, stop, look,...and ask yourself 'What do I need right now?'

Chapter Eight

New Mum Identity

Try completing the following sentence (in your head or written down): 'I am _____' with five different endings. Are your answers different to what you would have put before your baby was born?

Before having a baby we might have been able to make statements about ourselves such as:

'I am someone who needs nine hours sleep every night or I can't function.'

'I am a good friend who never misses a birthday.'

'I am always last to leave a good party.'

'I am good at my job.'

However, after having a baby many of the statements that we would have taken as 'true' suddenly don't apply anymore. This can lead to something akin to an identity crisis, where some of us struggle with knowing who we really are anymore. Some mums can feel as if having a baby means putting their 'real' lives on hold and others that being with their baby *is* their whole life. Some of us may swing between the extremes, depending on stress levels and tiredness.

Some articles and books suggest making sure you connect with friends, make time for yourself, or have adult conversations. These suggestions, although well meant, can fuel the idea that there is something to 'fix'. For some of us, the idea that we 'should' be connecting with friends and seeking out adult conversation can feel a pressure. For others it can feel like a relief to be given 'permission' to seek time away from all things baby related.

However you are feeling at the moment about your new-mum identity, it is worth remembering that it won't be like this forever, whatever stage you are at right now. Most of us start the journey as mothers of new-borns dealing with the shock of being on call 24 hours a day. But soon we are mums of toddlers and then of school age children, and so it continues to change as our children grow and families evolve.

Having a baby can have a huge impact on almost all aspects of our lives, so it's not surprising our sense of self shifts and might need some reconsidering and revising. The following comments show a range of reactions to the issue of 'mum identity' and illustrate some of the ways in which other mothers have grappled with their own sense of self after their baby's birth.

***

I remember looking in the mirror a few days after giving birth and being almost shocked 'I' was still there. How could I still look the same? How could I look so much like me when everything was so totally, radically different?

Whenever I tried to speak to my friends about how I was feeling about being a mother it sounded so odd. It sounded like I wasn't happy being a mum and that's not the case. I wanted to be able to tell them how hard it was, but couldn't find the right words.

I am pleased that I am the one who gets to stay at home. But sometimes I am jealous of my partner getting to have his morning drive to work on his own, to listen to the radio in peace, to choose when he has a tea break, and to talk to his colleagues about non-baby stuff.

I felt complete when I finally had my baby. So much of my identity had already been focused on being a mum because we spent so long trying to get pregnant. I never felt any loss of myself, but lots of friends did.

My life totally changed after having my baby and I was in a fog for the first year. I look back at the pre-baby me with some sort of fond awe that I had all those hours and days to myself. Did I use them all wisely? Did I take advantage of that time?

I felt like I had more freedom and independence after my baby was born. To not have to go to work and be assessed by a boss; to not have to account for every minute and provide reports; to be able to have the whole day ahead and choose what to do.

I felt like I'd lost my freedom, independence, and sense of identity. My role as free spirit had been crushed. I was no longer the last in the pub, the one with the biggest hangover, the joker. I felt I was weighed down by the seriousness of being a mum. I couldn't see that I would ever get back the parts of me that were gone. Now my baby is older, I can see that actually I never lost who I was, I just had to put some things on hold, and becoming a mum has given me a chance to reassess my lifestyle. I can't now go out on spontaneous drinking sessions or take a last minute holiday with my mates, but that's ok.

As two women bringing up twins, I thought we didn't have to worry about becoming gender stereotyped, so it was a surprise to me how much I felt like an old fashioned housewife in the early weeks when my partner went off to work waving goodbye to me in my nightie, dishevelled at the door, holding two babies and surveying the mess of our house.

I never felt I lost part of my identity when I became a mum because I always had my faith.

I'd always wanted to be a mother, so I was surprised at how much of a shock it was to adjust.

I was worried I would have forgotten how to function in the work world. I felt my brain didn't work how it used to. But I needn't have worried. It all came back. I wish I hadn't worried about it and just embraced the journey and the baby brain; it was just that my focus was on being a mummy.

***

Exercise 7

What makes you smile? What makes you laugh? See if you can do any of the things that help you laugh or smile. Some ideas could be to watch a funny film or a clip of your favourite comedian on the internet. Do you have a friend who you often end up laughing with you could arrange to see or speak to? Maybe you like talking through old family times with a relative or playing a board game? It might be too much to make it to a comedy show, but if it's not, book an evening in, or set a date for yourself to go in six months or even a year's time. If you can't think of anything just try a smile right now. Sometimes just the act of smiling or laughing can help us feel lighter.

Chapter Nine

Relationships

Think for a moment how many relationships in your life have changed since you had a baby. If you have a partner, has there been any snappiness? Angry words? Sulking? Have you seen as much of your friends? Have you looked at your mum, dad or mother-in law with new eyes? What about the negotiating of new friendships, or baby and mum groups? Almost every relationship in your life is likely to be going through some re-adjustment.

If you are in a relationship you might find that there is less time to spend as a couple once a baby is in the mix. Less time to spend listening to each other, looking at each other, touching each other, and bonding with each other. There is now another person, who makes up for what they lack in size, with the amount of attention they need from the parents.

Alongside the new practical limitations on your relationship, the effects of tiredness also means that when you disagree over any parenting decisions (from which nappies to use to whether or not to have the baby in your bed) it can be harder to communicate reasonably. Having the intention to be as gentle as you can with yourself and each other during all these adjustments puts you in a good position for when tiredness and subsequent grumpiness kicks in.

The relationship with your own parents (whether they are alive and in your life or not) has to negotiate new territory now you are a mother too. How this feels can depends on your own childhood, your memories of childhood, how you have managed the shift from child to adult, and how your parents are adapting to being grandparents. For some women, it can be the relationship with their mother that can cause some of the greatest stress due to the complexities of mother-daughter relationships. For those who no longer have a mother in their lives, there can be fresh grief to cope with along with caring for a new-born. When we care for a baby we often think back to ourselves as babies and with that comes memories of how we were parented. If either or both of our own parents have died the pain can be raw again.

Our friendships are not immune to changes at this time either. There can be hidden dynamics between old friends when one has a baby; alongside congratulations and joy there may be feelings of resentment, envy, disappointment and frustration. The practicalities of meeting up suddenly have to be renegotiated too as it is harder to make spontaneous plans, after work drinks, long dinners out or weekends away.

Making new mum friendships can also be tricky. Having babies the same age can be an amazing bonding tool but as human beings we tend to seek out others and to compare ourselves to them. When we have a baby the urge to protect our baby can cause our social comparisons to go haywire and we can end up checking ourselves against others and falling short again and again which can be painful when we are surrounded by other new mums.

New mums can be dealing with so many

emotions, thoughts and processes yet so often we don't even stop to acknowledge them. This section has given a brief overview of just some of the complexities that may be affecting our relationships and the example quotes below illustrate more ways women's relationships have been affected after having a baby.

***

I started to rely on my mother-in-law in a way I never had to before. I was grateful she would happily hold the baby while I had a shower. She would turn up with a meal and although all my old annoyances with her were still there I learnt to be more humble about them. I realised I needed and wanted her, and could take the rough with the smooth.

I vividly remember the first mum and baby group I went to. It was in a church hall, tucked away just yards from my house, but I had never noticed it before. It was full of women who seemed totally at home and seemed to know each other. I know that wasn't necessarily the case, but at the time it was overwhelming.

I was in a cafe with my baby and my best friend. We had just been shown to the table and I turned to my friend and said 'shall I take him out the buggy or just leave him there?' She just looked at me and said 'I don't know, you're the mummy'. I suddenly felt so alone.

I was constantly snapping at my husband. I knew I was being mean to him, but I couldn't help it. It was as if I was blaming him for all the hard bits of being a mother. Maybe on some level I was.

It was less than an hour after the baby had been born. I looked over at my boyfriend holding this little bundle and I was totally floored. He was staring at our baby with a look I had never seen before. I could see all this love coming from his eyes. I felt like a strong mother lion and I felt this fierce protection over both of them.

I have found it hard imagining my mum looking after me when I was a baby. We don't have a close relationship, but I now realise how much she must have done for me.

When the health visitor asked me about contraception I looked at her like she was mad. I still felt bruised from birth, my breasts were leaking all the time, and we were both getting no sleep. We could just about manage some friendly words and the odd hug, sex was way down our list of priorities.

I genuinely thought about divorce. We just brought out the worst in each other.

My antenatal group was a lifesaver. We had so many park meet ups and even shared first birthday parties. All of us bonded really well and helped each out through bouts of mastitis, sleepless nights, teething, weaning, arguments with partners, negotiations with work and issues with the in-laws.

In the first few weeks of my baby's life I cried for the loss of my mum 15 years ago. It felt like the grief had been rubbed raw again.

I had been looking forward to having a group of friends with the same age babies, but our antenatal group didn't work out. There were a couple of strong personalities in the group and it seemed there was always just one way to do everything that didn't fit with me. The meet ups were about one-upmanship. After a couple of months the meet ups dwindled. I am friends with one other mum and I am glad for that friendship, but it's a shame we never really had a proper group like some people do.

***

Exercise 8
Do you remember the exercise about doing something just for you, from Chapter Four? Now is the chance to turn this towards someone else. Pick a friend, your partner, your dad, your mum, your mother-in-law, your dog, the post-person, or

whoever you want, and decide to do something for them, with the intention of expanding your focus of kindness from yourself to someone else. It can be something as simple as a big smile next time you see them, or making a cup of tea, asking about their day, ordering a small gift online, writing a card, or giving them a flower. It can be whatever you can manage right now. It might seem counter intuitive at a time when perhaps making a sandwich or having a shower feels nearly impossible, but one small act can make a difference to our mood. By reaching out and expressing kindness to someone else, your own wellbeing can be enhanced and your intention to be kind to yourself can be strengthened as well.

Chapter Ten

Expectations versus reality

It is normal to have hopes, dreams and expectations about our babies before they are born, but it is likely that reality will not match all of our imaginings. The pregnancy and birth rarely go exactly to plan, and from the moment the baby is born, she or he might challenge our preconceptions. It might be that your baby looks different to how you imagined she or he would, or is a different gender to what you expected. It might be that your feelings differ from what you imagined. Sometimes babies are born with temporary illnesses that can worry and shock us. Or they might be born with physical deformities, disabilities, or serious health problems that we didn't expect.

The difficulty with expectations is not in having them, but how we feel if reality falls short. It can be painful to lose hopes and dreams and feeling disappointment about anything to do with our babies may also lead to guilt or shame for feeling that way.

We often envisage how we will be as mothers and how our family unit will be. Sometimes our realities actually exceed our expectations and we manage better than we feared. But sometimes the reality is harder and messier than we imagined.

If our children are ill, or we have to change our lifestyle to help our children, we can end up with a sense of unfairness. We might feel that life itself is unfair, that it is unfair our children have to face pain, that it's unfair other people have healthy babies. We might ask 'why me and why my baby?' and then feel guilty for feeling bitter and hurting. It's human and normal to feel like this. It is part of the process to go through and it doesn't mean you are a bad person or a bad mother.

When there is a difference between your expectations and your reality it can be helpful to spend a few moments acknowledging it. Let yourself express that disappointment, surprise or sense of unfairness and if you can share your feelings with someone else that can help too. Below are some example quotes demonstrating the gap between expectation and reality for some mums and how they felt about that gap.

***

I wasn't expecting a purple baby. I kept repeating 'he's purple'. His colour changed quite quickly but I'll never forget my initial surprise at seeing him. I had never seen a new-born baby before.

I thought I would have this 'glow' of new motherhood, as if something would have totally changed and I would be suffused with some sort of shroud of peace and love. It definitely didn't feel like that.

I was taken to see the baby in the special care baby unit. I was wheeled me into a room full of glass cots, flashing lights, beeping equipment, tubes and wires. A doctor turned to me and asked 'Are you his mum?'. I said 'yes', but inside I was recoiling. I wanted to be anywhere other than that room. I wanted to be curled up in a bed somewhere. I wanted to be with the healthy baby I'd imagined. I wanted to never know about this room, this place and this pain.

I had expected some sleepless nights. I expected it would feel like when I had stayed up late working or pulled all-nighters at college. What I hadn't realised was that in those days I used to catch up. After a couple of nights partying I would get into my pyjamas at 7pm, loll on the sofa for an hour or two, and settle down for a nice 12 hours straight in bed. Ha. Not anymore catching up. I had not considered what that would actually feel like.

I didn't expect to hate my baby, but sometimes I did. It's taken me a while to accept that doesn't mean I am a bad mum it just means sometimes I am a tired emotional mum noticing the extremes of my emotions.

As a single mum one of my worries was how I

would manage if I got ill. I was scared of getting the flu or a stomach bug but when it happened it was ok. It reinforced for me the need to take everything one step at a time, there's no point worrying about what you can't control or predict.

Everything hurt me. Every happy post and baby picture on Facebook stung, I felt sensitive about other people's actions and words. If I didn't get a card, I thought it was because they couldn't handle the fact my baby was deformed, and if I got a cheery congratulations card, I felt they were dismissing my pain.

I'd been terrified about how I was going to manage. I had never even changed a nappy before. But it's actually not as bad as I thought it was going to be.

I didn't feel as if I could join in our NCT group's discussions. I felt as if I was on the outside because my concerns weren't 'just' about sleeping and feeding but about my baby's health.

I thought I would always be a patient, loving and caring mum. I knew I would be tired but I thought the love for my baby would overcome the tiredness. The reality is that I am not always patient and I don't always feel loving or caring. That has shocked me.

***

Exercise 9

Give yourself a gentle pat on the shoulder, just three little gentle pats, either right hand on left shoulder or the other way round. That's all. You could try giving yourself a few of these little shoulder pats any time of the day perhaps, especially when any sadness or difficult thoughts or feelings might be building, and you could do with some care. You could even try just doing it in your imagination if you are somewhere where it might feel odd to do it physically.

Chapter Eleven

Going Forward

As our babies grow, we will learn to say goodbye to every passing stage. How can we remember to be kind to ourselves when our toddlers are having raging tantrums, our tweens are saying they hate us, our teenagers are barely talking to us and eventually our 'babies' are heading out the front door for good? Our intention to be kinder to ourselves can be easily forgotten in the midst of every new stressor. Here are two final exercises designed to help you remember to be kind to yourself (however old your 'babies' are).

***

Exercise 10
This exercise can seem a little strange, but bear with it if you can. Hold one of your hands in your

other hand and just notice the feel of it's warmth and weight for a few seconds. Next give it a squeeze and say (in your head if it feels too weird to say out loud) 'lovely hands' or some other warm phrase that feels nurturing. You might notice other thoughts creep in like 'what a weird exercise' or 'what am I doing?'. If so, that's ok, just notice the thoughts gently and carry on. Take two deep breaths in and out noticing the breath entering and leaving your body. Let go of your hands and give them a big smile. Next time you leave you house as you push the buggy, drive the car, hold a small child's hand or even sit in a meeting, take a look at your hands and remember you matter and are worth sending kindness to.

***

Exercise 11

The idea for this exercise it to get a pack of post it notes (or paper and tape or tack) and write at least three (you could do more than three) nurturing messages to remind you of your intentions to be kind to yourself. Here are some examples of some phrases you could write:

- 'self-kindness'
- 'I don't have to be perfect'
- 'hello me'
- 'take a breath'
- 'and…. breathe'
- 'what do I need right now?'
- 'am I taking care of me?'
- 'what would my wisest kindest imagined person say to me now?'

Whatever you choose, stick them around your house as little reminders. Possible locations could be: inside the wardrobe door, on a drawer handle, on the bathroom mirror, by the kettle, toaster or oven, by the front door, by the TV or even on the handle of the buggy. The idea is that they act as little reminders to pay attention to yourself and what you need throughout the day.

***

As you near the end of this book perhaps spend a moment to think whether it would be helpful to carry any of the ideas with you as you continue your motherhood journey. Has anything especially resonated with you? Are there any exercises it would help to repeat regularly? The ideas and exercises have been developed to be used again and again. Sometimes what isn't helpful one day can work well another day (and vice versa) so it might be worth repeating the exercises and trying them on different days or different times of day.

Chapter Twelve

Additional Resources

In order to develop the ideas for this book I drew on a number of different psychological theories, models and research (as well as my own experiences and work with mums). If you have found the ideas in this book helpful and would like to learn more about some of the background theories and research, information can be found in the resources below. Some of the theories and ideas might not fit with your own beliefs. However, some may resonate and provide you with more useful ideas. If you are feeling especially low or anxious, speaking to your GP or health visitor can provide help and support. You wouldn't be alone in feeling that way or be the first mum to benefit from extra support, as so many of us struggle in all sorts of different ways.

Websites

www.self-compassion.org

www.compassionatemind.co.uk

Books

Cree, M. (2015). *The Compassionate Mind Approach to Postnatal Depression. Using Compassion Focused Therapy to Enhance Mood, Confidence and Bonding*. London: Robinson.

Davey, G., Cavannagh, K., Jones, F., Turner, L., & Whittington, A. (2012). *Managing Anxiety with CBT for Dummies*. Chichester: John Wiley & Sons Ltd.

Germer, C. (2009). *The Mindful Path to Self-Compassion*. New York: The Guilford Press.

Gilbert, P. (2009). *The Compassionate Mind*. London: Constable.

Kabat-Zinn, J. (1994). *Wherever You Go There You Are: Mindfulness Meditation for Everyday Life.* New York: Hyperion.

Morgan, A. (2000). *What is Narrative Therapy? An Easy to Read Introduction.* Adelaide: Dulwich Centre Publications.

Neff, K. (2011). *Self-Compassion. Stop Beating Yourself Up and Leave Insecurity Behind.* London: Hodder & Stoughton.

Williams, M., & Penman, D. (2011). *Mindfulness. A Practical Guide to Finding Peace in a Frantic World.* Great Britain: Piatkus.

Finally, if you've got any feedback, or comments please visit www.charlottehartleyjones.com or www.selfkindnessformums.com
I wish you all the best for the rest of your motherhood journey and hope that self-kindness can play a part to help you through the highs and lows to come.

Printed in Great Britain
by Amazon